Your World

Picnics

3-D Shapes

Linda Claire

We are going to have a picnic!

We see shapes.

We see cylinders.

We see cones.

We see spheres.

We see cubes.

Time to eat!

⚙ Problem Solving

It is a birthday picnic! Where are the 3-D shapes? Use *above*, *below*, *beside*, and *behind* to describe where they are.

1. Where is a cone?

2. Where is a cylinder?

3. Where is a sphere?

4. Where is a cube?

Answer Key

Answers will vary. Examples:

1. A cone is behind the girl's head.

2. A cylinder is beside the cake.

3. A sphere is below the lid of the jar.

4. A cube is above the purple present.

Consultants

Nicole Belasco, M.Ed.
Kindergarten Teacher, Colonial School District

Colleen Pollitt, M.A.Ed.
Math Support Teacher, Howard County Public Schools

Publishing Credits

Rachelle Cracchiolo, M.S.Ed., *Publisher*
Conni Medina, M.A.Ed., *Managing Editor*
Dona Herweck Rice, *Series Developer*
Emily R. Smith, M.A.Ed., *Series Developer*
Diana Kenney, M.A.Ed., NBCT, *Content Director*
June Kikuchi, *Content Director*
Véronique Bos, *Creative Director*
Robin Erickson, *Art Director*
Stacy Monsman, M.A., and Karen Malaska, M.Ed., *Editors*
Michelle Jovin, M.A., *Associate Editor*
Fabiola Sepulveda, *Graphic Designer*

Image Credits: All images from iStock and/or Shutterstock.

Library of Congress Cataloging-in-Publication Data

Names: Claire, Linda author..
Title: Your world : picnics / Linda Claire.
Description: Huntington Beach, California : Teacher Created Materials, [2018]
 | Audience: Grades: K to Grade 3.
Identifiers: LCCN 2017059891 (print) | LCCN 2018020790 (ebook) | ISBN
 9781480759664 (e-book) | ISBN 9781425856281 (Paperback)
Subjects: LCSH: Picnics--Juvenile literature.
Classification: LCC GT2955 (ebook) | LCC GT2955 .C53 2019 (print) | DDC
 394/.3--dc23
LC record available at https://lccn.loc.gov/2017059891

Teacher Created Materials

5301 Oceanus Drive
Huntington Beach, CA 92649-1030
www.tcmpub.com

ISBN 978-1-4258-5628-1